AS Physical Education
UNIT 2563

OCR

Module 2563:
Contemporary Studies
in Physical Education

Symond Burrows

Philip Allan Updates
Market Place
Deddington
Oxfordshire
OX15 0SE

tel: 01869 338652
fax: 01869 337590
e-mail: sales@philipallan.co.uk
www.philipallan.co.uk

ISBN-13: 978-1-84489-011-8
ISBN-10: 1-84489-011-2

This Guide has been written specifically to support students preparing for the OCR AS Physical Education Unit 2563 examination. The content has been neither approved nor endorsed by OCR and remains the sole responsibility of the author.

Printed by MPG Books, Bodmin

Environmental information
The paper on which this title is printed is sourced from managed, sustainable forests.

Contents

Introduction

■ ■ ■

Content Guidance

■ ■ ■

Questions and Answers

Introduction

About this guide

This guide is written to help you prepare for the Unit 2563 test, which examines the content of **Module 2563: Contemporary Studies in Physical Education**. There are three sections to this guide:

- **Introduction** — this provides advice on how to use the unit guide, an explanation of the skills required by Unit 2563 and suggestions for effective revision.
- **Content Guidance** — this summarises the specification content of Module 2563.
- **Questions and Answers** — this provides examples of questions from various topic areas, together with answers to these questions and examiner's comments on how they could have been improved. It concludes with a mock unit test — this provides examples of questions in the same style as those in the unit test. A mark scheme is included with guidelines to enable you to assess your answers and identify your strengths and weaknesses.

An effective way to use this guide is to read through this introduction at the beginning of your course to familiarise yourself with the skills required for AS Physical Education. Try to make a habit of following the study skills and revision advice offered in this section. It may also help to refer back to this information at regular intervals during your course.

The Content Guidance section will be useful when revising a particular topic because it highlights the key points of each subsection of the Unit 2563 specification. You may want to tick off topic areas as you learn them to make sure that you have revised everything thoroughly.

The Question and Answer section will provide useful practice when preparing for the unit test. This practice should increase your awareness of exam-technique issues and maximise your chances of success.

Finally, you should attempt the mock unit test and use the mark scheme to assess your answers.

The specification

In order to make a good start to Module 2563, it is important to have a close look at the specification. If you do not have a copy of this, either ask your teacher for one or download it from the OCR website — **www.ocr.org.uk**.

The specification describes the content of the modules and gives information about the unit tests. It is important for you to understand the following key terms used in the specification:

- **analysis** — a detailed examination to find the meaning or essential features of a topic
- **characteristic** — a feature or key distinguishing quality
- **definition** — a clear, concise statement of the meaning of a word
- **function** — the purpose or a specific role
- **initiative** — a new action taken to cause change
- **strategy** — a plan to achieve a particular goal
- **transition** — change or passage from one stage to another

The specification also provides information about other skills required in Unit 2563, such as the requirement to respond to and interpret visual material. Therefore, it is important to familiarise yourself with photographs and diagrams from various sections of the specification — for example, try comparing sporting images with recreational ones as part of your revision of key concepts.

Finally, in addition to looking at the specification, it would be useful for you to read the examiners' reports and mark schemes from previous Unit 2563 tests (these are available from OCR). These documents show you the depth of knowledge that examiners are looking for, as well as pointing out common mistakes and providing advice on how to achieve good grades.

Study skills and revision strategies

All students need good study skills to be successful. This section provides advice and guidance on how to study AS physical education, together with some strategies for effective revision.

Organising your notes

PE students can accumulate a large quantity of notes and it is useful to keep this information in an organised manner. The presentation is important: good notes should always be clear and concise. You could try organising your notes under main headings and subheadings, with key points highlighted using capitals, italics or colour. Numbered lists are useful, as can be the presentation of information in the form of tables or simple diagrams, for example:

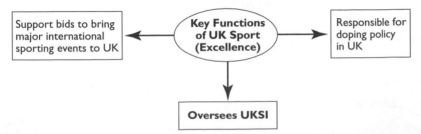

It is a good idea to file your notes in specification order, using a consistent series of headings, as illustrated below:

Module 2563: Issue analysis

Ethics and high-level sport — performer violence
There are a number of reasons why sports performers may become violent, including:
- retaliation against an opponent
- the will to win at all costs
- frustration at losing

At a convenient time after lessons, it is a good idea to check your understanding of your notes. If anything is still unclear, ask a friend to explain, do some further reading or ask your teacher for further help.

Organising your time

It is a good idea to make a revision timetable to ensure you use your time effectively. This should allow enough time to cover *all* the relevant material. However, it must also be realistic. For many students, revising for longer than an hour at a time becomes counterproductive, so you should allow time for short relaxation breaks or to exercise to refresh the body and mind. During spare moments, cue cards can be used to revise short snippets of information.

Improving your memory

There are several ways to improve the effectiveness of your memory. Organising Module 2563 material will help, especially if you use topic headings, numbered lists and diagrams. Reviewing and condensing your notes will also be useful, as will discussing topics with teachers and other students. Using mnemonics (memory aids) can make a big difference. For example, a mnemonic for the key characteristics of sport is:
- **S**erious
- **P**rowess involved
- **O**fficials present
- **R**ule governed/strict rules structures/national governing bodies
- **T**ime phased/strict time constraints

Revision strategies

To revise a topic effectively, you should work carefully through your notes, using a copy of the specification to make sure everything is covered. Summarise your notes to the key points using the tips given on note making above. Topic cue cards, with a summary of key facts and visual representations of the material, can be useful. These are easily carried around for quick revision. Finally, use the Content Guidance and Question and Answer sections in this book, discussing any problems or difficulties you have with your teachers or other students.

In many ways, you should prepare for a unit test like an athlete prepares for a major event, such as the Olympic Games. An athlete trains every day for weeks or months before the event, practising the required skills in order to achieve the best result on the day. So it is with exam preparation: everything you do should contribute to your chances of success in the unit test.

The following points summarise some of the strategies that you may wish to use to make sure your revision is as effective as possible:

- Use a revision timetable.
- Ideally, spend time revising in a quiet room, sitting upright at a desk or table, with no distractions (turn off your mobile phone!).
- Test yourself regularly to assess the effectiveness of your revision. Ask yourself: 'Which techniques work best?' 'What are the gaps in my knowledge?' Remember to revise what you *don't* know.
- Practise past paper questions to highlight gaps in your knowledge and understanding and to improve your technique. You will also become more familiar with the terminology used in exam questions.
- Spend time doing 'active revision', such as:
  - discussing topics with fellow students or teachers
  - summarising your notes
  - compiling revision cue cards
  - answering previous test questions and self-checking against mark schemes
  - reading the sports pages of newspapers or watching *Sky Sports News* or *Transworld Sport* to increase your knowledge of relevant, up-to-date sporting examples of contemporary issues (e.g. drugs controversies, National Governing Body initiatives and foul play in sport).

Revision progress

You might find it useful to keep track of how your revision is going by drawing up a table similar to the one below, including topics in the first column.

Module topic – sport and culture	Revised (N/P/F)	Self-evaluation (1–5)

• Primitive/tribal cultures
• Emergent cultures
• Advanced cultures
  – sport and commercialism
  – sport and politics
• Ethnic sports		

Complete column 2 to show how far you have progressed with your revision.

N = Not revised yet

P = Partly revised

F = Fully revised

Complete column 3 to show how confident you are with the topic.

5 = high degree of confidence

1 = minimal confidence — the practice questions were poorly answered

The table should be updated as your revision progresses.

The unit test

Unit Test 2563 consists of two compulsory structured questions. Mark allocations vary, but there are generally 3–5 marks for each of the first three parts of each question and up to 8 marks for the fourth part, which is often the potentially more difficult 'banded' question. The 8 or so marks are available to candidates who answer all the different elements of the question set. For example, in answer to a question on disabled participation in sport, maximum marks can only be obtained if the answer includes an analysis of:

- opportunity (e.g. money/cost)
- provision (e.g. access to facilities and specialist coaches)
- esteem (e.g. self-confidence free from discrimination)

If one section is answered poorly (or not answered), the answer cannot make the top band even if the answers to other parts of the question are exemplary.

There are 45 marks available in this test, which lasts for 1 hour and 15 minutes (giving you just under 1.5 minutes per mark). There are two *compulsory* questions. The questions may use pictures or diagrams as stimulus materials. If reference to the stimulus material is asked for in the question, you *must* refer to it in your answer. Often it can help with answers.

Lines are provided on which to write your answers and additional blank pages are sometimes available at the back of the question–answer booklet. You should avoid squashing your answer into the available space because this can make it difficult to read. Do not write answers in the left- or right-hand margin because these are for the examiner's use.

Questions may have some words emphasised. This is to draw your attention to key words or phrases that you need to consider in order to answer the question. Sometimes, questions are followed by 'structured headings'. This is to help you organise your response. Make sure you write the appropriate answer under the correct subheading.

There are a number of terms commonly used in the Unit 2563 exam. It is important that you understand the meaning of each of these terms and that you answer the question appropriately.

- **Compare** — point out similarities and differences.
- **Define** — give a statement outlining what is meant by a particular term.
- **Describe** — give an accurate account of the main points in relation to the task set.
- **Discuss** — describe and evaluate, putting forward the various opinions on a topic.
- **Explain** — give reasons to justify your answer.
- **Identify** — show understanding of unique or key characteristics.
- **State/give/list/name** — give a concise, factual answer.
- **What?/why?/where?/who?/how?** — these indicate direct questions requiring concise answers.

Whatever the questions style, you must read the wording very carefully, underline or highlight key terms or phrases, think about your response and allocate time according to the number of marks available. Further advice and guidance on answering Unit 2563 exam questions is provided in the Question and Answer section of this book.

The day of the unit test

On the day of the test, make sure that you have:

- two or more blue/black pens/pencils
- a watch to check the time
- water in a clear bottle to keep you hydrated

Make sure that you allow plenty of time to arrive, so that you are relaxed.

Read each question very carefully so that your answers are appropriate and relevant. Make sure that your writing is legible (you will not be awarded marks if the examiner cannot read what you have written). If you need more room for your answer, look for space at the bottom of the page or use the spare sheets at the end of the booklet. If you do this, alert the examiner by adding 'continued below', or 'continued on page X'.

Time is sometimes a problem. Make sure you know how long you have for the whole test. If you finish early, check your answers, adding more points to ensure you gain as many marks as possible. This is your one chance to impress the examiner — so take it!

Content Guidance

Module 2563 can be divided into six main topic areas:

- Key words for key concepts
- Issue analysis — sport in schools
- Roles of a coach
- Sport and culture
- Issue analysis — policy, provision and administration of sport, and the pursuit of excellence
- Issue analysis — sport and mass participation

You may already be familiar with some of the information in these topic areas. However, it is important that you know and understand this information exactly as described in the specification. This summary of the specification content highlights key points. Therefore, you should find it useful when revising for the Unit 2563 test.

In addition to summarising the specification content, this section includes useful examiner's tips, while at the end of some sections there is a list of points entitled 'what the examiner will expect you to be able to do'.

Remember that this content evidence is designed to support your revision and must be used in conjunction with your own notes.

Key words for key concepts

Towards a concept of play

Key features of play include:
- fun and enjoyment
- spontaneity
- simple or childlike behaviour
- flexible, self-agreed rules
- flexible, self-agreed time–space boundaries

Play sometimes fails to meet all these characteristics. For example, it is not fun if children argue or cheat.

The main function of play for a child is to master reality (i.e. what it is to take on an 'acceptable role' in society). Through play, children indirectly learn many things, including:
- physical skills, such as coordination
- social skills, such as making friends
- cognitive skills, such as decision making
- moral skills, such as fair play
- emotional skills, such as accepting defeat
- environmental skills, such as safety awareness

The key functions of play for an adult include escaping from reality. Play provides stress relief, relaxation and recuperation from daily duties.

Physical and outdoor education

PE can be defined as 'a formally planned and taught curriculum, designed to increase knowledge and values through physical activity and experience'. It has National Curriculum status as a compulsory subject from 5–16 years of age because it has a number of important functions in relation to pupils gaining such knowledge and values.

Aims of National Curriculum PE

The aims and objectives of National Curriculum PE can be achieved via set lessons. In addition, schools offer extra-curricular options for:
- sporting involvement (e.g. playing competitively for the school netball team)
- recreational involvement (e.g. open-access badminton club)

These provide further opportunities for the development of the national curriculum aims. Therefore, sport, recreation and education all co-exist in the school PE experience. This is summarised in the table below.

Knowledge/values	Examples
Physical and motor skills	Coordination; body awareness
Health and fitness	Physical activity in lessons; knowledge of the body; benefits of exercise
Preparation for active leisure	Encouragement and education about the benefits of continuing physical activity into adulthood
Personal value of self-realisation	Achieving success; increasing self-confidence and self-esteem
Socialisation and social skills	Making friends; improving communication skills
Leadership	Opportunities to lead or captain a group or team

Outdoor and adventurous education

Outdoor and adventurous education (OAE) is a compulsory part of National Curriculum PE. It can be defined as 'the achievement of educational objectives via guided and direct experience in the **natural environment**'. Examples include mountain walking and climbing. There is an element of **risk** involved in the natural environment, which sets OAE apart from other aspects of PE.

The purposes and functions of OAE are summarised in the diagram below.

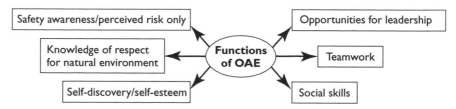

Despite its compulsory status as part of National Curriculum PE, OAE in most schools tends to be of relatively low quality, for example orienteering around the school grounds. There are a number of reasons for this, including:

- cost
- lack of qualified or motivated staff
- lack of time in a lesson
- parents and/or teachers deterred by the inherent risks

Physical and outdoor recreation

The term '**recreation**' can be defined as the 'active aspect of leisure'. It is entered into **voluntarily** during free time and individuals have a **choice** about which activities to take part in. Recreation is similar to play in its relatively unsophisticated nature, limited organisation and emphasis on taking part as opposed to winning. People take part in recreational activities to relax, to relieve stress and to improve their health and fitness. Opportunities arise to meet people and socialise in a relatively informal environment. Recreation is limited in terms of organisation and competition.

Outdoor recreation

Outdoor recreational activities take place in the natural environment. This gives people the opportunity to experience at first hand the aesthetic beauty of the country-side and to learn to respect and appreciate the natural environment.

For some individuals, outdoor recreation provides a sense of adventure. The adrenaline buzz from situations involving **real risk** (e.g. skiing off-piste during the time of an avalanche warning) is what makes recreation in the outdoors appealing to them, in addition to the other benefits.

Individuals may experience **perceived risk**. This means a feeling of danger when the situation is safe, for example when abseiling down the side of a rock face while wearing a safety harness and under the control of qualified instructors.

Sport

Sport is identified via a number of key features. It involves **competitiveness** (i.e. the will to win) and is **serious**, particularly at the top, elite level. **National governing bodies** (e.g. the Football Association) look after the interests of, and try to develop the popularity of, a particular sport. They also provide strict **rule structures** that are enforced in **competitions** by **officials**. Sport requires high levels of physical **skill** (prowess) and **effort** (endeavour) in order to succeed and gain the **extrinsic rewards**, such as trophies or money, that are on offer.

The levels of seriousness, commitment and skill in sporting involvement vary. Some individuals are talented enough to take part professionally (i.e. for a living). Others participate in sport as amateurs during their leisure time.

Sport is, therefore, different from recreation in that it is competitive, strict rules apply and extrinsic rewards are available.

Tip The more of these characteristics you can identify, the more likely it is that an activity can be classified as sport.

When participating in sport, performers can adopt various **codes of behaviour**, which can be viewed on a continuum:

Sportsmanship (functional)	Gamesmanship (dysfunctional)
• Treat opponents with respect • Fair play • Play within the rules or etiquette of the activity Example: kick the ball out of play if an opponent is injured — improves the atmosphere of the game	• Lack of respect for opponents • Use of unfair practices to gain an advantage • Often against etiquette of activity Example: playing on, despite an obvious injury to an opponent — could lead to ill-feeling

Comparing physical recreation with sport

The same activity (e.g. tennis) can be pursued as either recreation or sport. If tennis is played recreationally, there will be:
- flexible, self-enforced rules
- limited levels of organisation
- lots of enjoyment and fun
- fair play and sportsmanship
- low skill and commitment levels

As a sport, particularly at the highest levels, there will be:
- strict rules, with an umpire present
- high levels of organisation
- a serious, competitive atmosphere
- elements of sportsmanship and gamesmanship
- high skill and commitment levels

The performance pyramid

A pyramid structure can be used to illustrate a continuum of development from mass participation at its base through to excellence at the top.

What the examiners will expect you to be able to do

There is always a range of questions from the concepts section of the specification. They could require:
- listing or identifying key features or characteristics of a concept (e.g. play, sport or recreation)
- a comparison between different concepts (e.g. sport with recreation or play)
- the application of a variety of different concepts to a specified activity (e.g. swimming as play, sport, PE or recreation)

Tip Apply your knowledge of concepts to the question as appropriate and you won't go too far wrong.

Issue analysis: sport in schools

You have to be able to review and show your understanding of two current initiatives and strategies in school sport.

Development of sport in children

At **primary school** level there is **TOPSport** in England and **Dragon Sport** in Wales. In the **secondary school** sector, an awareness of **specialist sports colleges** is required. The involvement of **Sports Development Officers** at both levels is also important.

Various national agencies support the development of sporting activity in school children. The **Youth Sports Trust**, for example, has played a key role in providing **progressive pathways** through which children can develop. TOPS and Dragon Sport programmes have also played a key role in this, particularly in relation to providing child-friendly equipment and resources for a variety of different sporting activities. Primary school teachers can use these in conjunction with resource cards detailing quality ways of delivering practical sessions. To develop confidence further in delivering TOPS programmes, teachers and sports leaders are given quality training. The Youth Sports Trust is also involved in the School Sports Coordinators Programme (see below). It has a contract with the DfES to provide help and advice for schools applying for sports college status.

Sports colleges

Central government policies on school PE and sport have seen a number of initiatives put in place designed both to increase the numbers taking part and to raise standards of performance. Secondary schools can apply for **specialist status** in a variety of areas, including sport. A **sports college** is a secondary school that has been granted specialist status for sport. Financial benefits are gained from this, so sports colleges can afford excellent facilities and top-level coaching. More curricular and extra-curricular time for PE is often provided. Sports colleges form links with national governing bodies and the United Kingdom Sports Institute (UKSI) network in their specialist sport to support talented individuals (e.g. tennis at Burleigh Sports College and Loughborough University).

Sports colleges are also required to develop positive links with primary schools, special schools and the local community to provide opportunities for all to become active. Therefore, sports colleges have a key role in providing a regional focus point for excellence in PE and sport.

School Sports Coordinators Programme

School Sports Coordinators are often based at sports colleges and work to try to improve the quality and quantity of after-school sport and inter-school competition across their designated 'families' of schools. One way of doing this is to provide PE and sports courses for the ongoing professional development of teachers and other adults.

What the examiners will expect you to be able to do

Questions will be set asking for specific knowledge of initiatives in school PE and sport. You should be aware of:
- benefits of sports college status for pupils and the community in general
- key features of TOPS programmes

In addition, when more general questions are set in relation to mass participation and sports excellence, knowledge of relevant initiatives in school PE is required.

Roles of a coach

A coach performs a number of key roles to meet the many and ever-changing demands of the sports performers with whom they are involved:
- As an **instructor**, a coach gives **one-way communication** to ensure that the performers understand the rules and regulations of a sport.
- As a **trainer**, a coach works on **technique** and **fitness** to help performers meet the demands of their sport and to improve performance levels.
- The role of an **educator** includes working on the **ethics** and **morals** of a performer. In this role, the coach is interested in the **whole person** as an individual.
- As a **psychologist**, a coach works to ensure performers are at their 'optimum' mentally and neither too relaxed nor over-anxious as they prepare to compete.
- When a performer is injured, the coach takes on the role of **first-aider** by treating them appropriately.
- As a friend/social worker, a coach listens to performers' personal problems and tries to help them through difficult times.

What the examiners will expect you to be able to do

Questions on the roles of a coach come up relatively infrequently, but you need to prepare for them just in case. Knowledge of five or six key roles is required along with practical examples of each. The specification places particular emphasis on the roles of **instructor**, **trainer** and **educator**.

Sport and culture

Sport reflects the **culture** (traditions, customs, sports and pastimes) and **society** (interacting community) in which it exists.

Traditional and ethnic sports

Some traditional sports and festivals have survived over many years in **isolated rural** communities. Relative isolation allows local customs to continue. The **Highland Games** is an example of a surviving **multi-sports festival**. The Games reflect their **Gaelic heritage**. They have a number of key features and reasons for survival, which are summarised in the diagram below:

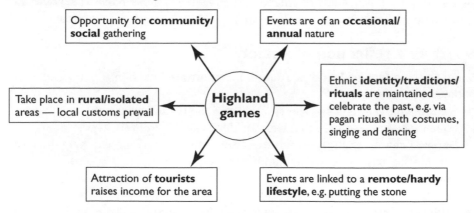

An example of a surviving **single-sport** occasion is the Ashbourne mob football match. This annual event takes place on Shrove Tuesday. In 2003, it was started by Prince Charles.

Tribal cultures

Tribal cultures are basic societies with relatively little technological and economic development. They lack sophistication and rely on a primitive way of life — for example, many still hunt for food.

Stages of development

Three stages of development have influenced life and physical activities in tribal cultures like that of the Samoans. The key features of these stages of development are outlined below.

Pre-colonialism

Pre-colonialism refers to the time before colonialists, such as the British, arrived.

- Activities were linked to the **natural** environment.
- Sports were linked to **ritual** needs (e.g. fierce stick-fights in praise of the gods).

Colonialism

During colonisation, British culture was imposed on the indigenous populations by schools, the church and the military.

- Christianity was imposed.
- English-style schools were opened, which taught the newly organised sports and games of late nineteenth century England, such as rugby.
- Traditional sports and pastimes diminished.

Post-colonialism

After colonialism, countries such as Samoa regained independence.

- Rugby continued to be played because its rugged, physical nature appealed to Samoans.
- Rugby was also a way of unifying villages and it was an ideal medium for inter-village rivalry and celebration.
- Aspects of ethnic identity re-emerged, such as the Samoan haka. This war-dance calls upon the gods of war. It links the pre-colonial pastimes with modern sport.

Sport as a reflection of society

Some features that explain how culture and sport are linked in tribal societies are outlined below:

- **Natural characteristics** — sports often used the natural environment with simple equipment and resources that were readily available from the land.
- **Survival characteristics** — sport exercises activities necessary to help the group continue to exist, for example hunting skills.
- **Functional characteristics** — some activities serve a useful purpose, for example wrestling contests to select a leader.
- **Ritual characteristics** — sports can fulfil a religious or sacrificial need, for example dancing to appease the gods and rituals performed on special occasions.
- **Community and social characteristics** — sport involves gatherings and social mixing and promotes a sense of community or group identity.

Emergent societies

An **emergent society** is one that has progressed beyond its tribal origins but is still classed as **less economically developed** than advanced nations. An emergent country has relatively low levels of economic and technological advancement.

Sporting success

Emergent countries such as Kenya use sporting success (e.g. in long-distance running) for various reasons:

- **Nation building** — success improves international status, recognition and respect from the rest of world because sport shows the emergent country off in its best light (i.e. the **shop-window effect**).
- **Integration** — sport is a powerful way of bringing tribes and communities together.
- **Appeasement**, **stability** and **social control** — the country is less politically volatile because people feel happier due to the nation's sporting success.
- **Role models** — heroes are created to which the population can aspire.
- **Health** — fitness and health are improved through participation in sport.
- **Defence** — participation in sport creates a fitter fighting force to defend the nation.

Sport development

An awareness of *how* emergent cultures such as Kenya achieve relative success in the world of sport is required. Emergent cultures develop sport in particular ways:

- **Disproportionate funding** — investment in sport is out of proportion, for example, to health and education.
- **Elitist and selective** — the initial focus is on top performers (the elite) in one high-profile sport; for example, the Kenyan long-distance runners are consistently successful at the Olympic games, which are watched all over the world.
- **Low technology** — the sport selected is cheap, simple, natural and easy to fund.
- **Role models** — world and Olympic champions become national heroes and others seek to emulate them.

Now that the primary motive of achieving international success in running has been achieved, the Kenyan government has begun to broaden its focus and a wider variety of sports is being developed. Cricket, soccer and basketball are all becoming more widely played in Kenya.

Advanced cultures

Sport and commercialism

Some key words and phrases linking sport and commercialism are explained below:

- **Capitalist model of sport** — this involves private ownership for **profit**, e.g. in the USA.
- **Commercial purposes** — sport is a media product to be bought and sold, advertised, sponsored or used to sell other products. Sport is big business; it needs to entertain to sell.
- **Win ethic** — with high rewards at stake, 'win at all costs' attitudes dominate sport.
- **The American dream** — this is the idea of 'rags to riches'; anyone can achieve success, wealth or status through their efforts.

- **Recreation** — free-time active leisure opportunities are theoretically available to all for escape and refreshment.
- **National interest** — sport is used to promote national pride and identity, for example through winning medals or hosting the Olympics.

Sport and politics

In communist countries such as Cuba and China (and the former USSR) sport has been closely linked to **politics**. This is illustrated by the **shop-window effect**, i.e. propaganda. Sporting success in international events such as the Olympics was used (and sometimes still is used) to illustrate the superiority of communism to the rest of the world. Positive, successful sporting role models promoted the country's status, while internal problems, such as the general health and poor quality of life of most citizens, were ignored.

Other key features of sport in communist cultures include:

- **functional characteristics** — sport is an instrument of the state, increasing the readiness of the population for work or war.
- **collectivism** — the needs of the nation are put above those of the individual and everyone works together to achieve the same communist goals.
- **centralism** — all decisions are made at the centre, i.e. by the government.

What the examiners will expect you to be able to do

There are always questions linked to different parts of the 'sport and culture' section of the specification.

- Ethnic sports questions either require you to identify the key features of events such as the Highland Games or to give reasons for the survival of ethnic sports.
- Questions linked to characteristics of sport in tribal cultures occur quite frequently. They require you to be able both to list and to explain such characteristics.
- Questions on emergent cultures, such as Kenya, occur often. They link mainly to strategies for success (i.e. how?) and the reasons for sport being so important to such countries (i.e. why?).
- Perhaps the most difficult questions require you to identify and compare the key features of 'sport and politics' (e.g. China) and those of 'sport and commercialism' (e.g. USA).

Tip The key terms you need to know in relation to 'sport and culture' are identified and explained above. You need to learn them and apply them to the question set!

Issue analysis: policy, provision and administration of sport, and the pursuit of excellence

- Policy refers to government initiatives.
- Provision refers to, for example, facilities and coaching.
- Administration of sport refers to its structure and funding.
- The pursuit of excellence means trying to achieve the highest performance standards.

Sporting organisations

The sporting organisations described below work in partnership to develop performers in the pursuit of excellence. For example, national governing bodies (NGBs) link closely to the UK Sports Institute (UKSI), which is overseen by UK Sport and also supported by Sport England. The UK has a decentralised system in which power and control are held locally by individual coordinating organisations.

UK Sport

The roles of UK Sport include:
- focusing on excellence and elite sport in the UK
- overseeing the UKSI
- responsibility for doping control in the UK
- attracting major sports events to the UK, thereby promoting UK international status
- distributing lottery money to support top-level performers or to build facilities
- involvement in the 'more medals' aspect of the World Class Programme

Sport England

Sport England is an example of a home-country sports organisation. Its roles include:
- involvement in the 'more medals' aspect of the World Class Programme
- distribution of lottery money to performers via the World Class Performance Programme
- distribution of lottery money to support the building of top-class facilities

National governing bodies

There are several NGBs, for example the Football Association. Roles of NGBs include:
- providing talent-identification schemes

- training higher-level coaches through professionalised coaching policies and a structure for progression
- providing sports science and medical support
- developing an elite league
- providing academies and centres of excellence in order to develop talent
- organising national competitions
- selecting and preparing national squads
- selecting performers for world-class funding

Sportscoach UK

Sportscoach UK is an example of a supportive agency. It is the only organisation dedicated to providing an infrastructure geared solely to developing better coaches. Its roles include:

- the development of professional coaching policies and attitudes
- the provision of coach education schemes
- the support of individual coaches through workshops and resources that cover a wide range of topics and can be applied to all levels of coaching
- the development of sports research projects

Elitism

Elitism involves the focus of resources on top performers.

Funding issues associated with elitism

- **Disproportionate funding** — funding of sports excellence is out of proportion. Some argue that a greater share of money should be invested in, for example, health and education.
- **Inadequate funding** — sporting success generates national pride and the feel-good factor. Others argue that there should be *more* funding so that we can compete more successfully with, for example, other European nations and Australia.
- **National lottery funding** — many millions of pounds of lottery money have been invested in elite sport since 1997. Money goes directly to performers via the World Class Programme. Funds are provided for both living and sporting purposes (e.g. travelling expenses and equipment). This enables many individuals to become full-time athletes and to be able to afford the best equipment and clothing necessary to develop the highest performance standards. The lottery also funds the building of specialist facilities for top-level sports performers, such as those found at the UKSI and English Institute of Sport (EIS) centres. Pressure on lottery funding is increasing, with less money being available for sport as lottery sales decline and more bids are submitted for it.

- **Sport Aid** — provides limited funds of a few thousand pounds to young, up-and-coming performers with a proven financial need. Without such aid they may not be able to afford basic equipment and travel expenses.

New initiatives designed to increase sporting excellence

United Kingdom Sports Institute

The UKSI aims to provide elite British performers with everything they need to compete and gain success in international sport, such as top-quality facilities, coaches, sports science technology and medical support at various centres in the UK.

English Institute of Sport

The EIS is split into nine regions with a network of centres throughout the UK (e.g. Loughborough and Sheffield). Top-level performers work in the best facilities with top coaches and medical support (e.g. the High Performance Coaching Programme).

Financial support for sport

Winning gold medals costs a lot of money! Increasingly, politicians have seen the vote-winning potential of international sporting success and have become more willing to invest in top-level sport and to finance increasing levels of participation among the general public.

Public sector funding of sport (i.e. funding by the state or the lottery), for example by the World Class Performance Programme, is a major source of financial support for top-class athletes in a wide variety of sports. Central government and local authorities also contribute funds to help athletes.

Private sector funding involves companies sponsoring a team, an event or an individual in the hope that sporting success will lead to a commercial return.

Voluntary sector funding is where individuals or clubs fund their own training and participation. NGBs are also involved and exist for the benefit of their members.

Possible sources of funding for elite, up-and-coming performers in Britain include:
- the World Class Performance Programme (lottery)
- sponsorship and private companies
- Sports Aid
- NGBs
- trusts and charities
- parents and families
- part-time or full-time work

Types of sponsorship

Some examples of types of sports sponsorship are shown in the diagram below.

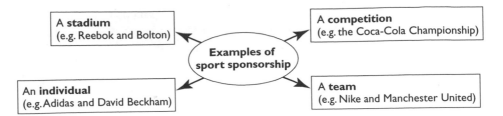

Sports sponsorship: reasons for and against

Sports sponsorship is the provision of money, or other support, to gain increased recognition for a product.

For	Against
Provides finance (e.g. motor racing)	Minority sports miss out
Increased revenue attracts top-level performers	Sport may have to accept intrusive demands of sponsors and television
Individual sponsorship allows full-time training	Sponsors (e.g. alcoholic drinks manufacturers) may give an unhealthy image to a sport

Ethics and high-level sport

Some attitudes to sport are summarised below:

- **Amateur attitudes** — taking part is more important than winning; fair play.
- **Professional attitudes** — win at all costs. With high rewards at stake, foul play is more evident in professional sport.
- **Win-ethic analysis** — the win-at-all-costs attitude can be good. Some individuals view this as essential for success in modern-day sport. Other people have a negative viewpoint, believing that the true spirit of fair competition is lost as individuals do whatever it takes (e.g. using drugs) to win.

Violence in sport

Violence by sports performers

Violence by performers means aggressive acts outside the rules of the sport. Causes and solutions are outlined below:

Cause of violence	Solution
Win-at-all-costs attitude; high rewards at stake	Educate on ethos of fair play; coaches encouraging sportsmanship
Frustration with poor decisions made by officials	Use of video technology to adjudicate on decisions (e.g. in rugby)
Following poor role models	Promotion of positive role models
It is in the nature of the game (e.g. rugby)	Harsher penalties for offenders

Violence by spectators at sporting events

Football hooliganism is an example of spectator violence.

Cause of violence	Solution
Too much alcohol consumed	Control or ban alcohol sales
Organised gangs	Use of police intelligence to combat gangs
Poor policing and lack of segregation	Improvements in policing and stewarding
Abusive or racist chants	Use of CCTV to identify troublemakers; harsher punishments; campaigns such as 'Kick racism out of football' and 'Kick it out'

Corruption

Major cities of the world see hosting the Olympic games as a positive, hugely beneficial honour. However, the bidding process for the Olympics has led to problems of corruption and bribery, as illustrated by the Salt Lake City scandal. Evidence was provided that a number of IOC members were given gifts (e.g. funding for the private education of their children) in return for their votes.

Performance-enhancing drugs and sport

Some reasons why athletes take drugs, together with possible solutions, are shown in the table below.

Causes	Solutions
Pressure from coaches or peers	Coordinated education programmes for coaches and athletes, highlighting the moral and health issues associated with drug taking
Win-at-all-costs attitude; high rewards at stake	Use of positive role models who stress the anti-drugs message but are still successful (e.g. Athens Olympic gold medallists Darren Campbell and Kelly Holmes)
Belief that all other athletes are taking them	Stricter, more rigorous random testing with greater financial investment
Lack of deterrents; perceived low risk of being caught	Stricter deterrents; harsher penalties for those caught

What the examiners will expect you to be able to do

Questions on sports excellence occur quite regularly, mainly in relation to key **organisations** and **initiatives** designed to promote and develop elite-level performers in the UK. A clear, concise knowledge of the key functions of UK Sport, Sport England, the

Youth Sports Trust and Sportscoach UK in relation to excellence is required. In addition, you should be able to talk about the impact of initiatives such as lottery funding, UKSI, EIS and specific governing body developments, such as talent identification programmes and appointments of performance directors (e.g. UK Athletics). Specialist sports colleges, with their emphasis on sport and high levels of coaching and facilities, should also be revised.

Ethical issues in sport should be understood in relation to causes and possible solutions. If a question is asked about solutions to the continued problem of drug usage in sport, it is important to answer the question set and not just write as much as you know about different types of drugs and their functions!

Issue analysis: sport and mass participation

The idea behind mass participation in sport is that everyone should have the chance to take part as often as they would like. However, reality does not always match the principle of equal opportunities in 'Sport for All'.

Initiatives to increase participation

Home country organisations

Sport England is a key organisation involved in raising participation levels among the general population. The aims of **more people** and **more places** are being implemented through a variety of schemes.

The more people initiative is being promoted by:
- Active Schools — TOPS/Activemark and Sportsmark are encouraging active participation in schools.
- Active Sports — this provides lottery funding for facilities and equipment for nine targeted sports, including athletics and basketball, to help school-aged children achieve more from their chosen sport.
- Active Communities — this encourages increased participation in sport by all sections of the community.

More places are being provided by:
- more efficient management of facilities
- lottery funding, which enables the building of more facilities for sport and recreation

Special interest groups

Women's Sports Foundation (WSF)

The WSF has a commitment to improving and promoting opportunities for women and girls in sport at all levels, by influencing changes in sports policy, practice and culture.

The key functions of the WSF are:
- to campaign for change to combat inequality in sport (mass participation)
- to raise the profile of British sportswomen, for example through national awards ceremonies and by working closely with the media
- to advise other organisations on women's sporting issues
- to promote the benefits of an active lifestyle (mass participation)

Disability Sport England

The key functions of Disability Sport England are mass participation and excellence. Mass participation is being encouraged by:
- working to improve awareness of, and the image of, disabled sport
- educating the general public about the capabilities of the disabled
- promoting the benefits of sport and recreation to the disabled
- encouraging disabled people to play an active role in the development of their sport

Excellence is being achieved by:
- working with other organisations to identify talent
- developing a national scouting programme
- staging national championships for specific sports

National governing bodies

Key functions of NGBs, such as the All England Netball Association, are:
- to encourage participation at all levels, including grass-roots
- to organise local competitions
- to plan and coordinate support programmes for affiliated clubs

Sportscoach UK

The key functions of Sportscoach UK are:
- to support new coaches with courses, resources and study packs
- to coordinate the Coaching for Teachers initiative, which aims to improve the standard of sports coaching in schools

Factors limiting the implementation of initiatives

There are constraints that limit the chances of people participating in sport regularly. These constraints may be based on opportunity, provision or esteem.

Opportunity refers to factors that affect the chance to take part, including:
- the attitudes of friends
- not having enough money to pay for the sport
- lack of time because of family or work commitments

Provision refers to more tangible features that influence participation, such as:
- lack of specialist facilities or access to such facilities
- lack of specialist equipment
- lack of appropriate activities (e.g. adopted sports for the disabled, such as wheelchair basketball)

Esteem refers to the perceptions held by others of an individual or group. Factors connected with esteem that limit participation in sport include:
- lack of self-confidence, low self-expectation and fear of rejection
- bullying
- discrimination (i.e. unfairness; imbalance of power between groups)
- lack of positive role models and low media coverage

Tip It is important to link appropriate constraints to particular special interest groups. For example, lack of time is more likely to be an issue for young mothers (because of work and family commitments) than it would be for an elderly person.

Socioeconomic and other factors

A number of factors that affect participation in sport are shown in the following table:

Factor	Reason
Friends	Peer group influence
Family	Parents and siblings as role models
Government	Funding for sport
School	Both positive and negative sporting experiences at school can affect lifetime attitudes to participation in sport
Socioeconomic status	Income and employment status affect the type of participation
Race and religion	Some ethnic groups have a negative attitude towards sport
Gender	Women take part in physical activity less regularly than men
Age	Over 50s and school leavers take part less regularly in physical activity than adults under 50 or children still at school
Disability	Some disabled people suffer from low self-esteem or stereotypical myths that limit participation

Sport and subcultures

A range of minority groups is covered by this issues analysis section of the Unit 2563 specification.

Social class and wealth

Social status, income and level of education all influence participation in sport. Evidence indicates that people from lower socioeconomic backgrounds tend to show a low level of participation. The reasons for this could include:
- the cost of participation
- low levels of health and fitness
- low self-esteem
- lack of opportunities
- few role models from a similar background in dominant positions
- a dislike of the dominant middle-class culture that surrounds certain sports, for example golf and hockey

Women

The participation by women at all levels of sport is significantly lower than that of men. Reasons for this include:
- lack of self-esteem, self-confidence and self-respect
- stereotypes and myths (e.g. the idea that it was harmful for women to take part in sport)
- restrictive/unappealing PE programmes for girls in schools (e.g. lack of choice of activities or of kit to wear)
- fewer female role models and less media coverage
- lower funding and fewer sponsorship opportunities

Ethnic minorities

We live in a multicultural, multiracial society. However, racism, unfair treatment and discrimination still affect the participation by some ethnic minority groups in physical activity and sport. Other factors that have a negative effect on participation include:
- few black or other ethnic-minority decision makers and organisers in sport
- stacking — the placing of ethnic minority individuals into similar positions in a team
- myths and stereotypes about the capabilities of certain ethnic groups to perform in certain sports or positions — for example, not placing these individuals in central/decision-making positions
- greater emphasis on education than on sport — some ethnic groups give sport a lower priority in comparison with gaining educational qualifications

Sport and the disabled

Reasons for low participation

A number of reasons have been put forward to explain discrimination against people with disabilities that prevents them from pursuing sport and physical activity. These include:

- attitudes and assumptions (e.g. the idea that disabled individuals don't want to do sport)
- myths and stereotypes (e.g. the idea that participation in sport is harmful to the disabled)
- inadequately designed environments
- lack of self-esteem
- few specialised coaches

Solutions to low participation

A number of possible solutions to low participation levels among disabled people have been put forward. These include:

- national disability sports associations cooperating to promote the benefits of sport for the disabled
- emphasising positive images of disabled people in sport
- improving access to facilities
- raising awareness of the abilities of specialist athletes with disabilities, for example through the paralympics
- adapting and modifying sports, for example by using larger, smaller or brighter balls
- providing suitable competition
- providing suitable facilities
- improving funding of facilities and elite performers
- more training of specialist coaches

Sport and the elderly

Elderly in this context refers to people over 50 years of age, since this is a target group of the Sport England campaign.

Reasons for low participation

A number of reasons have been put forward to explain lack of participation in sport among the elderly. These include:

- low self-esteem ('sport is for youngsters!')
- physical restrictions and poor health
- lack of choice of appealing options
- few older role models and less media coverage
- lack of transport
- poor PE experience

Solutions to low participation

A number of possible solutions to low participation levels among the elderly have been put forward. These include:

- re-educating the elderly about the benefits of sport and physical activity
- providing transport
- reducing or subsidising entrance fees
- campaigning for more media coverage of sporting events for veterans

Young people

Many of the points that have been made with respect to the elderly can be adapted to answer questions about young people — for example:

- reliance on parents for transport
- cost of participation
- poor PE experience

Roles of the media

The media (e.g. newspapers, TV, radio and the internet) have various roles — informing, educating, entertaining and advertising — in relation to sports coverage.

Information

Examples of information available through the media include:

- live coverage about what has happened or is happening in sport (e.g. results or latest scores on teletext)
- forthcoming fixtures and events (e.g. draws for major events detailed in newspapers)

Education

Media roles in education include:

- increasing public knowledge of global sports issues (e.g. use of drugs and hooliganism)
- improving understanding of tactical formations (e.g. use of the 4–5–1 formation in football) and rule changes in a sport (e.g. the offside rule changes in football)

Entertainment

Media roles in entertainment include:

- helping people to enjoy their leisure time by consuming sport as live entertainment
- filling the gaps in the action with lively discussion, action replays and player interviews
- providing an insight into the private lives of sports stars

Advertising

Media roles in advertising include:

- helping to generate income for sport (e.g. there are opportunities for sponsors to advertise their product around grounds and on performers' clothing)
- attracting sponsors to sports that have the most media coverage, such as football. Minority sports, such as netball, tend to be overlooked.

- promoting sports to make them more popular (e.g. during the 2004 Olympic games, British success in badminton and boxing resulted in increased participation in these sports in the UK)

What the examiners will expect you to be able to do

Questions on mass participation in sport occur frequently. You may be asked to state initiatives of organisations such as Sport England that are designed to increase participation.

Another key requirement is to be able to relate factors limiting participation in sport to particular special-interest groups. To access higher marks, answers to this type of question should be given under each of the following three headings: opportunity, provision and esteem. This is because questions on this topic area sometimes occur as 'banded questions' with high mark allocations.

Clear distinctions between the different roles of the media are required, with practical examples to back up your answers.

Questions
&
Answers

This section of the guide contains questions that are similar in style to those you can expect to see in Unit Test 2563. The questions cover the six areas of the specification identified in the Content Guidance section.

Each question is followed by an average or poor response (Candidate A) and an A-grade response (Candidate B).

You should try to answer these questions yourself, so that you can compare your answers with the candidates' responses. In this way you should be able to identify your strengths and weaknesses in both subject knowledge and exam technique.

Examiner's comments

All candidate responses are followed by examiner's comments. These are preceded by the icon *e* and indicate where credit is due. In the weaker answers they point out areas for improvement, specific problems and common errors, such as vagueness, irrelevance and misinterpretation of the question.

This section concludes with a mock Unit 2563 test accompanied with a mark scheme. Once you have completed your revision and worked through the sample questions on pages 37–51, you should try to complete the mock test under exam conditions. This means within the allowed time of 1 hour 15 minutes, in a silent environment, without reference to books or notes.

The mark scheme is provided so that you, or perhaps a teacher, can mark your responses. The potential difficulty here is deciding if a point is relevant when the exact wording of the mark scheme has not been used. You should also be aware that a particular point on the mark scheme may only be awarded once, even if a number of alternative answers are given. For example, 'cheating/rule breaking/legality' in relation to reasons for not taking drugs could all come under the same marking point.

There are 45 marks available in Unit Test 2563. Below is an approximate guide to enable you to compare your mock exam performance with final exam grades:
- 36 or more — A
- 31–35 — B
- 26–30 — C
- 21–25 — D
- 17–20 — E
- less than 17 — N

Question 1

Key words for key concepts

(a) **PE teachers aim to develop their pupils' knowledge and values. Identify values and benefits to be gained from a positive school PE experience.** (4 marks)

(b) **Play is often considered to be an educational experience. What can children learn through play?** (4 marks)

(c) **What are the main characteristics of sport?** (5 marks)

Total: 13 marks

■ ■ ■

Candidates' answers to Question 1

Candidate A

(a) Having a positive PE experience may encourage you to take up sport when you are older ✓. This can improve your health and general well-being ✓. Having a good experience can also help encourage your children to participate in sport.

> *e* The first two sentences earn marks as they are linked to the 'preparation for leisure' and 'improved health' values of PE. The final sentence is vague and confusing. The answer is too brief and lacks a range of different points. Candidate A scores 2 marks.

Candidate B

(a) A positive PE experience can lead to:
- the development of physical skills ✓
- health benefits ✓
- knowledge of the rules of a sport ✓
- help in getting a job or career in sport ✓
- an improvement in self-confidence ✓
- making friends and improving social skills ✓
- knowledge of tactics used in a sport

> *e* The first six points are all worth a mark. The final point about tactics is too similar to the earlier point about rules to be credited. This answer is written in an examiner-friendly way with a brief introduction and the key points listed as bullets. More points have been made than there are marks available, to try to ensure full marks are earned. Candidate B scores all 4 marks.

Candidate A

(b) Children can learn how to play fairly and respect the rules of a game ✓. They can learn about sportsmanship and accepting defeat. They also learn basic skills, such as throwing and catching ✓.

> *e* This is an example of an answer that is factually correct but focuses too much on one point — fair play. The second sentence repeats the first, so a mark cannot be

awarded. Without the practical example, the 'basic skills' point may not have been awarded because 'skills' could relate to physical, mental or social development. Candidate A scores 2 marks.

Candidate B

(b) • Children can learn how to interact with others ✓.
  • They learn fundamental motor skills by playing with such things as balls ✓.
  • They learn cognitive skills by problem solving ✓.
  • They learn how to cooperate and work together as a team ✓.
  • When making up their own games, they learn creative skills ✓.
  • They learn how to play safely ✓.

  e All six points are relevant and answer the question in a clear and succinct manner. Use of practical examples is further evidence of good exam practice, as is the fact that more points have been made than there are marks available. Candidate B scores all 4 marks.

Candidate A

(c) Sport is played professionally at high levels ✓. People such as Wayne Rooney earn lots of money from playing football for a living. He is my role model. I want to be like him because he plays at a high level for my favourite club. Some of the skills he produces on the pitch are fantastic which again makes me want to be like him ✓.

  e Although the use of practical examples to illustrate your understanding is to be encouraged, in this case too much focus on one person has limited the number of marks gained. Repeating the point about a professional playing for high rewards at a high level means only 1 mark can be gained because the characteristics are so similar. Reference to high skill levels gains a second mark. A variety of points should have been made in answer to this relatively simple question. Candidate A scores only 2 of the 5 available marks.

Candidate B

(c) Sport has a number of characteristics, such as:
  • competitiveness and the will to win ✓
  • rules ✓
  • high fitness demands ✓
  • governing bodies (e.g. the FA) ✓
  • use of specialist equipment ✓
  • officials that make decisions

  e Just enough relevant points are made to gain maximum marks. The final point cannot be awarded a mark because it repeats the point about 'rules'. It would have been a good idea to make one or two more points, in case of vagueness or more repetition. Missing out on maximum marks on relatively easy questions can make a significant difference to the final grade achieved. Unless a specific number is asked for in the question, always make more points than there are marks available. Candidate B scores all 5 marks.

e **Overall, Candidate A scores 6 out of 13 marks; Candidate B scores 13.**

Sport in schools

(a) **TOP Sport in England is an example of a primary school initiative.**
   Describe TOP Sport. (4 marks)
(b) **The pursuit of excellence is a major contemporary issue in sport.**
   How are sports colleges helping in the pursuit of excellence? (4 marks)

Total: 8 marks

■ ■ ■

Candidates' answers to Question 2

Candidate A

(a) TOP Sport is a series of initiatives for children aged from 18 months to 18 years. These range from TOP Tots to TOP Sportsability. They aim to develop skills and fitness through schooling. As the schemes increase, more analysis and coaching becomes involved.

> *e* The points made are irrelevant and vague. The question requires a description of TOP Sport, which is one of the TOPS programmes. This should be the focus of the answer. However, Candidate A focuses on describing the range of TOPS programmes available. To make sure that you answer the question set it might help to highlight key words or phrases in the question before starting to write your answer. Candidate A does not score.

Candidate B

(a) TOP Sport is supported and developed by the Youth Sports Trust ✓. It is designed to support teachers in their delivery of National Curriculum PE ✓ to 7–11 year olds ✓. Training is provided for teachers to deliver TOP Sport ✓. Specially adapted equipment bags ✓ are given to teachers to help them deliver TOP Sport. Teaching cards with lesson ideas on them are also provided ✓.

> *e* Candidate B has answered the question set and included many relevant points on TOP Sport. More correct points are made than the maximum mark available, which is good exam practice. Candidate B scores all 4 marks.

Candidate A

(b) Sports schools such as Millfield are very important in promoting excellence. They offer scholarships to talented performers who have the opportunity to pass lots of exams at the same time as improving skills. If you go to a sports college like Loughborough, you are guaranteed to work in excellent facilities with brilliant coaches.

> *e* All of this answer is irrelevant and Candidate A fails to score. Sports colleges are clearly identified in the specification as a state secondary school initiative that can

lead to specialist status for sport, with many benefits including the development of excellence-level performers. Millfield is a private school, while Loughborough is a university of higher education. A common cause of irrelevant answers is lack of revision in a particular topic area, so candidates resort to a 'best guess' response. While giving an answer is preferable to leaving a gap, it is more advisable to familiarise yourself with all areas of the specification through a planned revision schedule.

Candidate B

(b) Schools with sports college status aim to raise standards of performance at school level ✓ by providing opportunities for gifted and talented performers ✓. Links to the local community help to increase standards in local clubs ✓. Sports colleges employ high-level coaches ✓ and give more time to the delivery of sport both in lessons and after school ✓.

> *e* This is an excellent answer, which focuses on the main requirement of the question — the link between sports colleges and excellence. Candidate B scores full marks. Sometimes, students simply write everything they know about a topic, which, if the content is irrelevant, could earn them no marks. For example, in answer to this question some students might write about ways in which sports colleges increase participation, rather than how they develop sports excellence. As well as not earning marks, this would waste valuable time.

> *e* **Overall, Candidate A did not score; Candidate B gains all 8 marks.**

Roles of a coach

**(a) The roles of a coach are many and varied. Describe the following roles:
instructor, trainer and educator.** (3 marks)

(b) List two roles of a coach other than those of instructor, trainer and educator. (2 marks)

Total: 5 marks

■ ■ ■

Candidates' answers to Question 3

Candidate A

(a) Instructor — coaches instruct performers to do things
Trainer — trainers train performers to improve ✓
Educator — coaches educate performers

> *e* A common problem with low achievers is repetition of words from the question, particularly if they are unsure of alternative wording. The only mark awarded is given as a 'benefit of the doubt' (BOD) mark because there is a link to coaches training performers to *improve*. Candidate A scores 1 out of 3 marks.

Candidate B

(a) Instructor — the coach tells ✓ performers what to do (e.g. safety rules).
Trainer — the coach informs and discusses ✓ a performer's diet and training programme.
Educators — the coach has a two-way relationship with sports performers ✓ and teaches them about fair play.

> *e* This answer provides an excellent description of the three key roles of a coach and includes practical examples. The answers are succinct and give the relevant detail required for maximum marks.

Candidate A

(b) A coach as an instructor tells performers what to do. As a trainer, he/she improves performers' fitness.

> *e* This is all irrelevant to the question set and fails to score.

Candidate B

(b) Two other roles of a coach are first-aider ✓ and psychologist ✓.

> *e* This is a succinct answer, giving two relevant roles.

> *e* Candidate A scores 1 mark; Candidate B scores all 5 marks.

Sport and culture

(a) Define each of the following words or phrases:
   (i) culture
   (ii) ethnic identity
   (iii) colonialism   (3 marks)
(b) Individual countries approach sport in different ways for different reasons.
   Identify characteristics of:
   (i) sport and the 'American dream'
   (ii) sport as a 'shop window'   (6 marks)
(c) Other than nation building, identify and explain characteristics of sport
   in emergent countries.   (5 marks)

                                                           Total: 14 marks

■ ■ ■

Candidates' answers to Question 4

Candidate A

(a) **(i)** Culture is where you are brought up.
   (ii) Ethnic identity is your background, which gives you an identity.
   (iii) Colonialism involves colonials going to war and taking over a country.

   e The answer to part (i) is vague and lacks the clarity needed to gain a mark. In part
   (ii) the candidate repeats a term given in the question (i.e. identity) and fails to give
   a clear enough answer. In answer to part (iii) the candidate shows some limited
   understanding of the idea of taking over a previously independent nation by a
   dominant power. However, the response is too vague to earn a mark. Candidate A
   fails to score.

Candidate B

(a) **(i)** Culture is how a society lives — for example, its norms, attitudes, customs and
   traditions ✓.
   (ii) Ethnic identity is what makes a person or group unique — for example, race
   and customs ✓.
   (iii) Colonialism is basically empire building. This involved countries, such as
   England, taking over other nations and imposing their sports and way of life
   on them ✓.

   e There is 1 mark available for each acceptable definition or explanation of the terms
   asked. There is a tendency among students to leave a gap if unsure of a term. This
   should be avoided — you have nothing to lose by making an educated guess.
   Candidate B's answer explains all three terms clearly and correctly and scores all

3 marks. Although not necessary in this case, some concise examples are also given. Such development of an answer is the kind of information you should give if each part of the question were worth 2 marks, rather than 1.

Candidate A

(b) (i) Sport and the American dream:
- In the USA anyone can achieve success ✓.
- You can go from rags to riches.

(ii) Sport as a shop window:
- Sport is used for political reasons ✓.
- If you can win, it helps politicians.

e These answers are too brief and lack the understanding that, hopefully, would have been evident if the candidate had revised this section of the specification more thoroughly. In answer to each question part, a single point is made which is then repeated. Different points are required! Candidate A earns 2 marks.

Candidate B

(b) (i) There are a number of important characteristics of the American dream, including:
- wanting to win and be the best — the win ethic ✓
- earning lots of money, because sport is seen as a commodity to be bought and sold ✓
- being based on the capitalist principles of a free market ✓
- everyone taking part ✓

(ii) Key characteristics of sport as a shop window include:
- sport being used as a political tool ✓
- competing to try to win for the benefit of your country, not just for yourself ✓
- being based on socialist or communist systems ✓
- the idea that sport can be used to keep the population happy, despite problems, such as lack of food, that may be present ✓

e This shows how a question sub-divided into two parts should be answered. A similar amount of detail should be given in each part of the answer. This will give a balanced answer with a chance of gaining full marks. Aim to make four or five points in each part of the answer, in case one or more points are vague, irrelevant or repetitive. This is the type of question you should return to at the end of the test if you have time. If you are unsure, include the point, because the principle of positive marking means you cannot *lose* a mark if a point is wrong. Candidate B gains maximum marks.

Candidate A

(c) Kenya is an example of an emergent culture that uses sport for nation building. The government puts a lot of money into sport to produce good athletes. When they win, it brings recognition and sporting events to the country, which in turn brings money to the economy. Success also creates role models that children try to be like ✓. Health is improved when people are encouraged to run and exercise ✓.

e The start of this response focuses on aspects of nation building (e.g. economic benefits), which is irrelevant to the question set and will not gain marks. Underlining or highlighting the phrase 'other than nation building' in the question might have prevented the candidate from writing such irrelevant material. The 2 marks gained in relation to 'role models' and 'health' are fine as they both identify and explain key features of sport in emergent countries.

Candidate B

(c) Characteristics of sport in emergent countries includes:
- being selective — focusing on one sport, such as long-distance running in Kenya ✓
- being high profile — this sport is competed in at World and Olympic levels ✓
- being low-tech — a cheap sport like running is appropriate ✓
- integration — sport encourages people to work together ✓
- social control — sport is seen as a positive alternative to crime ✓
- defence — defence of the country is improved as many soldiers become fitter through running ✓
- disproportionate funding

e This is a well-structured answer that identifies *and* explains clearly the key characteristics of sport in emergent cultures. The first five of the six correct points made earn the maximum 5 marks. The final point, 'disproportionate funding', would not be given a mark because the question specifies 'identify and explain' and no explanation is given.

e **Overall, Candidate A scores 4 marks; Candidate B scores 14 marks.**

Question 5

Sports excellence

(a) Explain, in relation to the performance pyramid, what is meant by 'sports excellence' and list three different functions of UK Sport that are designed to promote excellence in the UK.   (4 marks)

(b) The winning of more medals is affected by many factors. What are the possible effects on elite performance of:
- funding (e.g. sponsorship/National Lottery)
- the UKSI (United Kingdom Sports Institute)
- the media (e.g. television and newspapers)   (9 marks)

(c) Despite harsher penalties and better testing procedures, some sports performers still take performance-enhancing drugs. Identify reasons for this and explain why the fight against drugs in sport must continue.   (6 marks)

Total: 19 marks

■ ■ ■

Candidates' answers to Question 5

Candidate A

(a) Excellence is being the best at the elite level of the pyramid ✓. To develop people to the top of the pyramid, UK Sport is building more facilities and training more coaches. It also gives out lottery money to help performers develop to the top ✓.

    e A good, logical start is made, with excellence linked to the word elite in relation to the pyramid. The answer then becomes vague. UK Sport has clear functions in relation to sports excellence in the UK, which are covered in the Content Guidance section of this guide. Unfortunately, many candidates struggle to recall these functions and to write about them in exams! This question asks for a specific number of functions — three — so in this case it is very important that the first three functions you state are correct. Candidate A scores 2 marks.

Candidate B

(a) Excellence is identified at the top of the sports pyramid with performers of very high standards ✓.

    UK Sport focuses on this excellence level and has a number of functions in relation to it, including:
- the distribution of lottery money to top-level performers through, for example, the World Class Programme ✓
- overseeing the UKSI ✓
- promoting the international status of the UK by attracting major international events to this country ✓

    e Candidate B scores full marks. This question requires precise knowledge of key facts, which are often not expressed well by students. This answer is restricted to three key points, as asked. If this is the case in a question, it is advisable to make a quick list of points that you feel are relevant and then decide which points are most likely to earn you marks.

Candidate A

(b) Funding increases the provision of specialist facilities where the elite can train ✓. It also helps them buy essential specialist equipment ✓. If they want to go warm-weather training in the winter, lottery money or a sponsor can help pay for this ✓.

The UKSI provides funding for elite performers which helps cover the cost of travel, coaches, and competition entry fees. Each centre has a specialist sport, such as the Manchester Velodrome for cycling.

The media can have both positive and negative effects on elite performers. Role models are presented to young people who inspire them ✓. The media promote majority sports, such as football, which get lots of coverage while minority sports, such as netball, are overshadowed ✓.

Media coverage can also promote bad role models and encourage drug taking to become an elite performer.

e The funding answer is good as three relevant points are made, scoring 1 mark each. In this kind of high-mark question, more points could perhaps have been made supplying more detail and illustrating a wider understanding of the issues involved. The answer referring to the effects of the media is adequate, but repetition of the point about role models (positive and negative) limits the marks. It would have been better to make a different relevant point. The answer referring to the effects of the UKSI is full of incorrect and irrelevant material. To gain high marks in this type of 'banded' question it is essential to give detailed, correct answers to each part of the question. This is a Level 2 answer, scoring 5 out of 9 marks.

Candidate B

(b) Funding can help athletes devote themselves full-time to a sport ✓. It helps them to be able to afford the best equipment ✓ and to train in the best facilities ✓ with the best coaches ✓ (e.g. Sport England's World Class Programme) ✓.

The UKSI offers top-level performers the chance to work with top-level coaches ✓ in the best facilities ✓, alongside performers at a similar high level who will inspire better performance ✓. Sports scientists are available to analyse and develop performers ✓. In addition, medical support and dieticians are there to help top-level performers keep fit and healthy ✓.

The media can affect top performers because having a great deal of coverage can influence sponsorship opportunities ✓. More people are encouraged to take up a sport and work towards excellence if it gets lots of media coverage ✓. The media can encourage top performers to do their best and hype up a team or individual. This can either work for or against them — it worked for the rugby World Cup winning England team ✓. Creation of positive role models, such as Kelly Holmes, encourages people to aspire to be like them ✓.

e This is an excellent top-band (i.e. 7–9 marks) answer. The candidate gives balanced and detailed answers to all three parts of the question. The inclusion of some practical examples shows clear understanding of the requirements of the question. Candidate B scores full marks.

Candidate A

(c) There are a number of reasons why performance-enhancing drugs are still taken, including:
  • pressure from the coach ✓
  • friends encouraging you to do so
  • the win-at-all-costs attitude ✓

The fight against drugs should continue because taking drugs is illegal ✓ and it is cheating. It is dangerous to health ✓ and may have adverse side effects.

e There are elements of good exam technique here. The answer is structured into two separate parts and there is an attempt to make clear, concise points in a bullet-point format, with apparently more points than there are marks available. However, a number of the points that are similar are regarded as 'repeats' of points already made. For example, the first two points are both about pressure; the second two are about ambition. Candidate A scores 4 marks.

Candidate B

(c) There are many reasons for taking drugs, including:
  • muscle-building and increasing strength ✓
  • losing weight or recovering from injury ✓
  • extrinsic rewards and fame on winning ✓
  • ineffective testing methods ✓
  • poor deterrents and punishments ✓
  • because others are taking drugs ✓

Reasons to fight drug taking include that:
  • it gives an unfair advantage ✓
  • it lowers the status of a sport (e.g. weight-lifting) ✓
  • it gives negative role models ✓
  • it is cheating ✓

e In a two-part question such as this there will be a sub-maximum of 3 or 4 marks available. Therefore, a minimum of four points should be made for each part. Candidate B makes ten relevant points, six in the first part and four in the second. The answer is balanced, concise and examiner-friendly as it is clearly structured and the separate points are easily distinguished. The first four points earn the sub-maximum 4 marks; the maximum of 6 marks is achieved by the two initial points in the second part of the answer.

e **Overall, Candidate A scores 11 out of 19 marks; Candidate B scores full marks.**

Sport and mass participation

(a) Explain each of the terms 'opportunity', 'provision' and 'esteem' in relation
    to mass participation in sport. (3 marks)
(b) Why might elderly people be unable to participate in sport or recreation? (6 marks)
(c) Home country sports councils, such as Sport England, aim to get more people
    involved in sport. Other than TOP Sport or Dragon Sport, identify recent
    schemes and campaigns aimed by Sport England at increasing participation in
    sport in the UK. (4 marks)

Total: 13 marks

■ ■ ■

Candidates' answers to Question 6

Candidate A

(a) Opportunity is how much free time ✓ you have to participate.
Provision is how good or widely available sporting facilities are ✓.
Esteem — if you are very quite, then you may find it hard to fit into a team.

e The Unit 2563 test sometimes has answers structured in a similar way to this, with
a term from the question followed by space for the answer. Therefore, each answer
must be specifically related to the word or phrase given. Candidate A gives correct
explanations of 'opportunity' and 'provision'. The final explanation is too vague and
also contains a spelling mistake ('quite' should read 'quiet'). Candidate A scores
2 marks.

Candidate B

(a) Opportunity — some sports, for example golf, are too expensive ✓. Can you afford
it? ✓
Provision — does your local area provide the facilities ✓ you need?
Esteem — if you are ashamed of your figure or get embarrassed ✓ because you
can't play sport, then you might not want to take part.

e All three terms are explained well, each scoring the available mark. The last point
in relation to 'esteem' is linked to the idea that people lack self-belief. This answer
is slightly longer than the others and may not fit in the space provided in the
question–answer booklet. If this happens, you should continue your answer in any
extra space at the bottom of the page or on spare pages at the back of the booklet.
Make sure that you indicate clearly where the answer is continued, so that the
examiner can find it.

■ ■ ■

Candidate A

(b) The administration of sport for the elderly is poor. There are few agencies or NGBs that allow the elderly to participate in sporting activities. Some people would worry — what if something happened to them? Little funding ✓ goes into sporting or recreational activities for the elderly. As few wish to participate anyway, the demand to solve the problem is low. Elderly people are on pensions, so therefore don't have much money.

> *e* This answer is far too vague and repetitive to earn many marks. 'Worry if something happened' should be further developed and linked to ageing. *Reasons* for low demand by the elderly would also earn marks. For example, there are few role models, the choice of appropriate activities is limited and there is a lack of publicity. Candidate A scores only 1 mark.

■ ■ ■

Candidate B

(b) Elderly people may be unable to participate because of health problems ✓, such as heart disease, which could prevent them from running. They may not have the money ✓ or time to take part. They may not have a car ✓ to drive to sports centres. The elderly might lack self-confidence ✓, particularly if they have had a poor experience at school ✓. Instructors and coaches are often unclear about how to work with older people ✓. There is a general lack of media coverage ✓ of sport for the elderly, with fewer role models ✓ to copy.

> *e* Nine potential points are made of which eight are correct. Therefore, Candidate B easily earns all 6 available marks. The only point that is not correct is the reference to lack of time. This does not apply to most elderly people because they are retired. However, positive marking means that this mistake is ignored.

Candidate A

(c) Many sponsorship schemes have been set up for young sports teams. Many more young people would be likely to join a club if it had a well-known sponsor. Comic Relief is good at getting people active, as is the London Marathon. TOP Sport is also good at encouraging mass participation.

> *e* This answer fails to score any marks. In relation to the question set, the answer is both vague and irrelevant. The question asks for schemes and campaigns in which Sport England is involved. It does not ask for mass participation events and funding strategies to encourage people to become involved in sport and recreation. Also, the question specifically excludes TOP Sport.

Candidate B

(c) Many schemes have been set up to increase participation:

- School sports coordinators ✓ have been appointed and work at Sports Colleges ✓ to get younger children involved in sport.

- TOP Tots and TOP Play ✓ have been used to get young children interested in sport.
- 'More people' has three main parts to it: Active Schools ✓ (e.g. Activemark ✓), Active Sports ✓ and Active Communities ✓.

e Candidate B easily achieves the maximum 4 marks as a number of relevant points are made in relation to Sport England's 'more people' schemes. No explanation of these is required because the question asks only for identification (e.g. by a list) of schemes and campaigns linked to the aim of 'more people'.

e **Overall, Candidate A scores 3 marks; Candidate B scores 13 marks.**

**mock
paper**

Unit 2563

(1) (a) Ethnic sports, such as the Highland Games, continue to survive in the UK today. Give reasons for the survival of such activities. *(8 lines) (4 marks)*

(b) (i) The Women's Sport Foundation is the only organisation in the UK that is solely committed to improving and promoting opportunities for women and girls in sport at all levels. How does it try to achieve the aim of providing equal opportunities for women and girls in sport? *(5 lines) (3 marks)*

(ii) Recently, there has been some success in raising the levels of participation of girls in football. This has resulted in increasing provision for them to do so. Explain why this has occurred. *(6 lines) (3 marks)*

(c) 'Olympic hopefuls in drugs scandal!' Drugs scandals associated with top sports performers continue to make headline news. Explain the social reasons why elite sportsmen and women continue to take drugs, despite knowing the potential risks to their careers. *(7 lines) (4 marks)*

(d) Explain why swimming as an activity could be classified as *each* of the following:
- physical recreation
- physical education
- sport *(4 lines each) (7 marks)*

Total: 21 marks

■ ■ ■

(2) (a) Give an example of a national governing body of sport and list *four* of its key functions. *(5 lines) (5 marks)*

(b) In emergent countries such as Kenya, sporting success is pursued for a variety of political and social reasons. What strategies do emergent nations use to try to bring about sporting success? *(7 lines) (3 marks)*

(c) (i) Define 'sponsorship' and give examples of different types of sports sponsorship. *(6 lines) (3 marks)*

(ii) Explain why sports sponsorship may sometimes be negative for performers. *(7 lines) (4 marks)*

(d) The pursuit of sporting excellence is an important contemporary issue. Explain how Sports Colleges, Sport England and UK Sport are helping in the pursuit of sporting excellence. *(12 lines) (6 marks)*

Total: 21 marks

■ ■ ■

Mark scheme

Marking points for Question 1

(a) 4 marks for four of the following points:
- tradition — tradition/wish to retain continuity/passed from generation to generation
- religious — annual religious feast/festival occasion/ritual/celebration of past times/local event/religion
- Community — community get together/social occasion/people come together
- ethnic identity — keep or retain ethnic identity/keep or retain culture
- tourism — boosts tourist industry/brings visitors/money to area/media attention
- rural — relative geographical isolation
- social class — links to royalty/royal patronage/links to higher social classes

(b) (i) 3 marks for three of the following points:
- information — information/commissioning research/educating/advising on key women's sport issues (e.g. participation figures/trends/media coverage)
- promotion — create and promote best elements of good practice
- campaigns — campaigns to try to influence change (e.g. the Brighton Declaration on Women in Sport)
- initiative — such as WSF Women 'Get Set Go' (a sport leadership programme)/ Women into high performance coaching/young elite sportswomen's seminars
- magazine — *Women in Sport* magazine

(b) (ii) 3 marks for three of the following points:
- change in social attitudes/less negative peer pressure/now socially acceptable
- equal rights/equality of opportunity/Sex Discrimination Act (not general role changes)
- increased popularity with girls/demand for more teams and leagues
- increased media coverage
- National Curriculum/PE influence/acceptability as part of PE programme
- more women being placed at higher levels/role models
- NGB/Sport England initiatives (e.g. Active Sports)/equity initiatives

(c) 4 marks for four of the following points:
- win-at-all-costs attitude
- high rewards at stake/worth the risk
- pressure from coaches/peers
- expectations of nation
- belief that everybody else is doing it/level the playing field
- perceived beliefs, i.e. lack of deterrents/minimal fines or bans/minimal punishments/poor testing/inadequate testing/will not get caught/fear of losing/cannot win without drugs
- follow role models (bad examples from the past)

(d) The sub-maximum mark is 3; the maximum mark is 7.

Physical recreation:
- voluntary/choice/no pressure to participate
- outcome or result not important
- enjoyment/relaxation/stress relief/opportunity to be creative/fun
- health/fitness motive
- social/swim with friends
- some level of organisation

Physical education:
- lesson/taught by a teacher/part of National Curriculum
- teaching of skills/learning skills
- teaching knowledge of activity/acquiring knowledge of activity, e.g. rules or scientific principles
- values taught
- preparation for life, e.g. active leisure
- development of fitness/health

Sport:
- competitive/serious/result important
- extrinsic rewards
- governing body/strict rules
- high level of organisation/galas/competitions

Marking points for Question 2

(2) (a) 1 mark for either Football Association, All England Netball Association, Rugby Football Union or Lawn Tennis Association (the abbreviation or the full name is acceptable).
4 marks for four of the following key functions:
- maintain rules/regulations of the sport
- promote the sport/seek media coverage
- organise competitions/leagues
- increase participation/grass roots
- discipline performers
- funding/control finances of the sport
- inform/advise clubs
- provision for excellence (e.g. World Class Programme)
- train coaches/officials
- administration/appoint officials
- liaise with other organisations (e.g. Sport England)

(b) 3 marks for three of the following points:
- selection/excellence pursued in a limited range of sports
- disproportionate/unequal funding of one sport
- role models to inspire youngsters

- high-profile Olympic sports chosen
- low technology/simple/cheap/natural sports chosen

(c) (i) 1 mark for:
- provision of funds or other support to individuals, teams or events in order to get a favourable return/publicity for a product

2 marks for two of the following types:
- kit/equipment/sportswear provision
- ground/facility/pitch sponsorship
- performer support (e.g. travel/competition costs)
- event/league sponsorship
- player of the match/series sponsorship

(ii) 4 marks for four of the following points:
- temptation to cheat because of high rewards of success
- inequality of sponsorship/performers in minority sports get limited sponsorship
- control/exploitation by sponsors
- media intrusion/loss of privacy
- insecurity/sponsorship may be withdrawn
- unhealthy image (e.g. if the sponsor is associated with alcohol)

(d) Points to look for in this levels-marked (banded) question (see explanation below):

Sports colleges
- raising of standards of performance at school level
- better quality teachers/coaches of PE/sport
- competition with peers
- regional focus for excellence/School Sports Coordinators
- links to community sports clubs
- improved quality of resources/facilities
- links to UKSI/NGBs
- more time for delivery of sport/PE

UK Sport/Sport England:
- more medals aspect of World Class Programme
- government/lottery funding distributed to elite athletes
- runs Athlete Career Education UK/gives careers advice
- runs anti-doping programme/promotes ethical standards of sport
- runs/oversees UK Sports Institute/English Institute of Sport
- attracts major events/improves UK international profile as a sporting nation

Levels
Level 3 (5–6 marks)
- A well-developed answer
- An answer showing sound knowledge and understanding of the roles/links between sports colleges, UK Sport and Sport England in relation to sports excellence

- Developed discussion/a well-structured answer

Level 2 (3–4 marks)

- A developed answer
- An answer showing knowledge and understanding of the roles/links between sports colleges, UK Sport and Sport England in relation to sports excellence
- Discussion may be limited/some structure is evident

Level 1 (1–2 marks)

- A simplistic/narrow/limited answer
- An answer showing limited knowledge and understanding of the roles/links between sports colleges, UK Sport and Sport England in relation to sports excellence
- A factual account; a disjointed answer lacking in structure

Quality of written communication

Unit 2563 gives 3 marks for quality of written communication, based on the following criteria:

High (3 marks)

- Well reasoned/ordered/clear, concise continuous prose
- A few errors of grammar, punctuation and spelling

Middle (2 marks)

- Reasoned/sound use of language
- Some errors of grammar, punctuation and spelling

Low (1 mark)

- Limited quality of language
- Noticeable/intrusive errors of grammar, punctuation and spelling